I0797615

INSIDE THE NFL

ARIZONA CARDINALS

by Ted Coleman

Abdo & Daughters
MIDDLE GRADE NONFICTION

An imprint of Abdo Publishing
abdobooks.com

ABDOBOOKS.COM

Published by Abdo Publishing, a division of ABDO, PO Box 398166, Minneapolis, Minnesota 55439.

Printed in China.
052025
092025

Cover Photos: Mike Christy/Getty Images Sport/Getty Images (Kyler Murray); Ralph Freso/Getty Images Sport/Getty Images (Larry Fitzgerald)
Interior Photos: Christian Petersen/Getty Images Sport/Getty Images, 4–5, 6; Norm Hall/Getty Images Sport/Getty Images, 7, 8, 63; Ross D. Franklin/AP Images, 9, 46, 52, 61 (top right); Abdo Publishing, 10–11; Bettmann/Getty Images, 12–13, 16, 19, 23, 24–25, 60 (bottom right); Pro Football Hall of Fame/AP Images, 14, 15, 17, 60 (bottom left); Chicago Sun-Times/AP Images, 18; AP Images, 20 (top), 21; Harry L. Hall/AP Images, 20 (bottom); Paul Cannon/AP Images, 22, 60 (top); Tony Tomsic/AP Images, 26, 27 (top); Vernon Biever/AP Images, 27 (bottom); Clifton Boutelle/Getty Images Sport/Getty Images, 28, 29, 61 (bottom left); Focus on Sport/Getty Images, 30; Focus on Sport/Getty Images Sport/Getty Images, 31, 37; Rob Schumacher/AP Images, 32–33; George Rose/Getty Images Sport/Getty Images, 34–35, 61 (top left); Greg Trott/AP Images, 36; Ken Levine/AP Images, 38; Jeff Haynes/AFP/Getty Images, 39; Roy Dabner/AP Images, 40; Mark J. Terrill/AP Images, 41; Gene J. Puskar/AP Images, 42, 51; Kevin C. Cox/Getty Images Sport/Getty Images, 43; Donald Miralle/Getty Images Sport/Getty Images, 44; Doug Benc/Getty Images Sport/Getty Images, 47; Gene Lower/Getty Images Sport/Getty Images, 48–49; Rick Scuteri/AP Images, 50; Kellen Micah/Icon Sportswire/Getty Images, 53; Michael Hickey/Getty Images Sport/Getty Images, 54–55; Gene Lower/AP Images, 56, 59, 61 (bottom right); Harry How/Getty Images Sport/Getty Images, 57; Shutterstock Images, 58

Editor: Haley Williams
Series Designer: Laura Graphenteen
Production Designer: Ebonee Estrella

Library of Congress Control Number: 2024948483

Publisher's Cataloging-in-Publication Data

Names: Coleman, Ted, author.
Title: Arizona Cardinals / by Ted Coleman
Description: Minneapolis, Minnesota: Abdo Publishing, 2026 | Series: Inside the NFL | Includes online resources and index.
Identifiers: ISBN 9781098296629 (lib. bdg.) | ISBN 9798384919148 (ebook)
Subjects: LCSH: Arizona Cardinals (Football team)--Juvenile literature. | National Football League--Juvenile literature. | Football teams--Juvenile literature. | American football--Juvenile literature.
Classification: DDC 796.333--dc23

CONTENTS

Arizona Cardinals quarterback Kyler Murray prepares to pass in the 2020 game against the Buffalo Bills.

CHAPTER 1

THE HAIL MURRAY

ARIZONA CARDINALS QUARTERBACK KYLER MURRAY LOOKED OVER THE Buffalo Bills' defense. Just 11 seconds remained in the Week 10 game of the 2020 National Football League (NFL) season. Trailing 30–26 and with time for about two more plays, Murray knew it was now or never.

The fact that the Cardinals were even in position to win the game was impressive. They had been down 23–9 early in the third quarter. Then Murray led a furious comeback, scoring two rushing touchdowns to put Arizona back in the lead before the fourth quarter began.

However, Buffalo retook the lead on a long touchdown pass with 34 seconds left. The Cardinals got the ball back, and over the course of 23 seconds, Murray advanced the Cardinals to the Bills' 43-yard line. But before the quarterback could attempt a game-winning play, Buffalo called a timeout.

LOOKING FOR A STAR

The Cardinals had originally planned to run a quick play to set up another one closer to the goal line. During the timeout, that plan changed. Arizona head coach Kliff Kingsbury had a message for Murray. He wanted the young quarterback to get the ball to wide receiver DeAndre Hopkins. Kingsbury told Murray, "If you like the look on Hop, take that shot."

Murray, *left*, talks strategy with Cardinals head coach Kliff Kingsbury during a timeout.

> **"IF YOU LIKE THE LOOK ON HOP, TAKE THAT SHOT."**
>
> **—KLIFF KINGSBURY**

Teams in a desperate situation late in the game often call a Hail Mary play. A Hail Mary usually involves sending multiple receivers into the end zone, lofting a deep pass in the area of one or more of them, and hoping one can make a play to score a touchdown. The Cardinals weren't calling

Wide receiver DeAndre Hopkins led the Cardinals with 115 catches and 1,407 receiving yards in 2020.

a Hail Mary in this situation. Kingsbury was trusting Murray to find Hopkins if the wide receiver got free in the end zone.

Murray was in his second season as the Cardinals' quarterback. After earning the NFL's Rookie of the Year Award in 2019, he used his special combination of skills in both running and passing to get the Cardinals off to their best start in years in 2020. It helped that Murray had a pair of the most consistent and reliable receivers in the game in Hopkins and Larry Fitzgerald. And the quarterback would indeed be looking for one of them on the next play.

HOPING TO FIND HOP

Murray took the snap. Almost right away, the Bills' pass rush forced him to scramble. Murray ran to his left as he scanned the field for open receivers. The play was taking a lot of time off the clock, meaning it would probably be Arizona's last of the game.

Using his elite athleticism, Murray escaped the oncoming defenders and scrambled toward the sideline to buy some time. This also allowed Hopkins to reach the end zone. With the Bills closing in fast, Murray stepped up and heaved a pass toward the goal line. However, Hopkins wasn't open. In fact, he was surrounded by three Bills defenders. But Murray knew what Hopkins was capable of.

Even as the defenders converged on Hopkins, he rose above them toward the ball. When the pass arrived, Bills players hit Hopkins from all angles. Yet he somehow gathered in the ball, brought it to his chest, and held on. Only when all the

Murray, *left*, breaks away from a Buffalo defender just before throwing the ball.

Hopkins, *in red*, outjumps three Bills defensive backs to make his incredible catch.

players hit the ground did the Bills realize Hopkins made the grab with two seconds left. His catch gave the Cardinals a 32–30 win and helped them improve to a 6–3 record. That was already more wins than they'd had in either of the previous two seasons.

Like many great plays, Murray's Hail Mary earned its own nickname. "The Hail Murray" became a legendary moment for one of the NFL's oldest franchises. And that history began more than 100 years earlier in a completely different part of the country.

PLAY OF THE YEAR

Successful Hail Mary passes don't happen very often. It is even rarer that they help win games. Kyler Murray's pass was the first touchdown on a Hail Mary to give a team a lead in the fourth quarter in five years. After the 2020 season, "the Hail Murray" was named Play of the Year at the annual NFL Honors.

NFL TEAMS MAP

NFC

NFC EAST

DALLAS COWBOYS

NEW YORK GIANTS

PHILADELPHIA EAGLES

WASHINGTON COMMANDERS

NFC WEST

ARIZONA CARDINALS

LOS ANGELES RAMS

SAN FRANCISCO 49ERS

SEATTLE SEAHAWKS

NFC NORTH

CHICAGO BEARS

DETROIT LIONS

GREEN BAY PACKERS

MINNESOTA VIKINGS

NFC SOUTH

ATLANTA FALCONS

CAROLINA PANTHERS

NEW ORLEANS SAINTS

TAMPA BAY BUCCANEERS

AFC

AFC EAST

- BUFFALO BILLS
- MIAMI DOLPHINS
- NEW ENGLAND PATRIOTS
- NEW YORK JETS

AFC WEST

- DENVER BRONCOS
- KANSAS CITY CHIEFS
- LAS VEGAS RAIDERS
- LOS ANGELES CHARGERS

AFC NORTH

- BALTIMORE RAVENS
- CINCINNATI BENGALS
- CLEVELAND BROWNS
- PITTSBURGH STEELERS

AFC SOUTH

- HOUSTON TEXANS
- INDIANAPOLIS COLTS
- JACKSONVILLE JAGUARS
- TENNESSEE TITANS

The Cardinals, *striped sleeves*, and the Chicago Bears are two of the NFL's oldest teams. They first played each other in 1920.

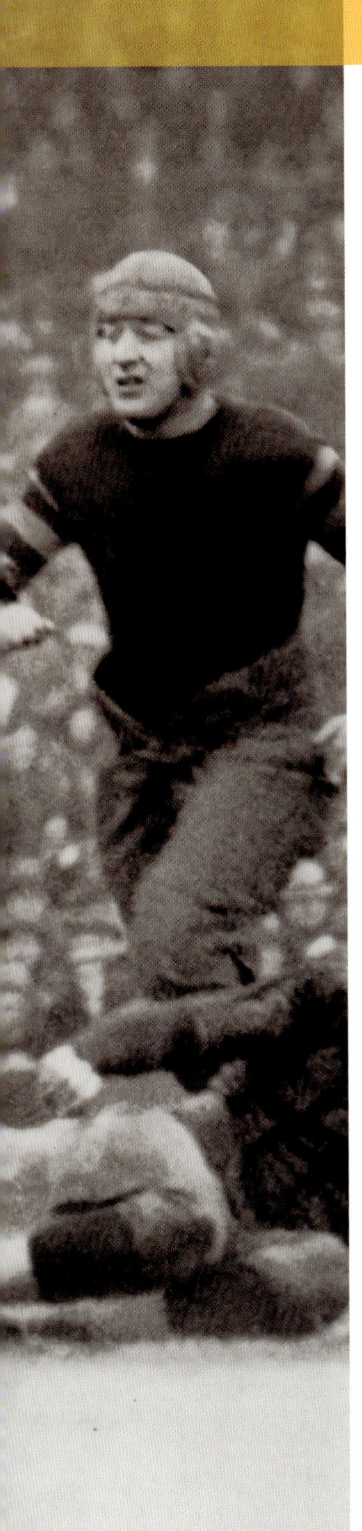

CHAPTER 2

CHICAGO'S OTHER TEAM

BACK WHEN THE CARDINALS WERE FOUNDED, IT WASN'T EVEN LEGAL TO throw the football forward. The Cardinals franchise traces back to 1898 with the founding of the Morgan Athletic Club in Chicago. Local contractor Chris O'Brien created the club as a neighborhood football team on the city's South Side. It would call the Windy City home for the next six decades.

The team took on the nickname Cardinals in 1901. That year, O'Brien acquired a set of used uniforms from the University of Chicago Maroons. The Maroons got their name from the dark red uniforms they wore. But these uniforms had faded into a lighter red. "That's not maroon, it's Cardinal red!" O'Brien exclaimed.

The uniform maybe wasn't what O'Brien expected, but it became both his team's color

The Cardinals had a record of 6-2-2 in 1920.

and nickname for good. At that time, the team was known as the Racine Cardinals, as it played at a field on Racine Street.

Professional football was still in its very early days at that time. Most of the Cardinals' opponents were amateur teams from around Chicago. In 1920, a few of those teams, along with some others from the Northeastern and Midwestern United States, met to form the American Professional Football Association (APFA). The fully professional league included the Cardinals as one of its 14 original members.

THE GLORY YEARS

There were a lot of changes in the early years of pro football. Teams came and went, moving, folding, and changing names. The Cardinals persevered, even with the changes around them. In 1922, the APFA changed its name to the NFL. The Cardinals also made a name change that year because a team from Racine, Wisconsin, joined the league. To avoid confusion, the team changed its name to the Chicago Cardinals.

The Cardinals were not alone in the city. While they played on the city's South Side at the stadium of the Chicago White Sox baseball team, the Chicago Bears football team played in the Chicago Cubs' baseball stadium on the North Side. The teams became natural rivals. The Bears were an early powerhouse in pro football, winning the 1921 league title and employing many star players. But the Cardinals had a star player of their own in Paddy Driscoll. Driscoll was a quarterback, running back, and sometimes punter who would go on to make the Pro Football Hall of Fame.

In 1925, the teams met on Thanksgiving Day at what's now called Wrigley Field. A then pro football-record 36,000 fans showed up, most of them to see Bears star running back Red Grange. But the Cardinals held Grange and the Bears to a 0–0 tie. The game was

Paddy Driscoll was the Cardinals' first star player.

The Cardinals had an early rivalry with running back Red Grange, *right*, and the Bears.

key in the Cardinals' championship hopes that season. In that era of the NFL, there was no Super Bowl. There weren't even playoffs. Whoever finished with the best record won the championship.

In December of that year, the Cardinals hosted the Pottsville Maroons in a snowstorm. Pottsville won the game to clinch the NFL's best record. However, the league later determined the Maroons had played an unauthorized game on their schedule. The title was then awarded to the Cardinals in one of the most controversial decisions in NFL history.

HISTORY MADE

In 1926, Driscoll left the Cardinals to join the Bears. This marked the beginning of a general downturn for the Cardinals. From 1926 to 1946, the team recorded just three winning seasons. However, this era did include important historical moments for the team and NFL.

In 1929, the Cardinals played the first night game in NFL history. The team traveled to Rhode Island to play the Providence Steam Roller at Kinsley Park Stadium. The game was played under newly installed lights, and the ball was painted white for extra visibility. The Cardinals didn't miss a beat as they shut out the Steam Roller 16–0.

Running back Ernie Nevers scored 26 rushing touchdowns in three seasons with the Cardinals.

The 1929 season was also the first in Cardinals history played under new ownership, as O'Brien sold the team to a local doctor named David Jones. Jones made some efforts to improve the team, including bringing on star running back Ernie Nevers to play and eventually coach. Nevers scored an NFL-record 40 points in a 40–6 win over the Bears in 1929. However, the Cardinals didn't see a lot of success before he retired in 1932.

That same year, Jones found himself as a guest on the yacht of Charles Bidwill, a Chicago lawyer who was also the co-owner and vice president of the Bears. The two talked about how Jones's

"WHY DON'T YOU SELL THE TEAM TO CHARLEY?"

—VIOLET BIDWILL

team was struggling on and off the field. Since the Cardinals weren't winning, they attracted few fans and were losing money. After hearing this, Bidwill's wife, Violet Bidwill, jokingly said to Jones, "Why don't you sell the team to Charley?"

CARDINALS TRAILBLAZER

While Black players were never officially banned from playing in the NFL, they were rare in the league's early days. For all but two games from 1927 to 1929, Cardinals lineman Duke Slater was the only Black player in the NFL. While that made Slater noteworthy, his play on the field really made him stand out. Slater played on both the offensive and defensive line and was selected as an All-Pro seven times between 1922 and 1931. While doing that, he graduated from law school. After his playing days, Slater eventually became a judge in Chicago.

Duke Slater played for the Cardinals from 1926 to 1931.

Bidwill had wanted a pro football team of his own for years. So when Jones said he would sell the team for the right price, Bidwill jumped at the opportunity. They agreed on a price of $50,000, with Bidwill giving Jones $2,000 in cash on the spot.

Bidwill was a big believer in the future of pro football. He bought the Cardinals even though they were a poor team that lost money. He believed that over time, the team would be a good investment. It proved to be a smart decision. The Bidwill family still owned the team more than 90 years later, and by then it was valued at more than $4 billion.

The Card-Pitt combination team, *in white pants*, faces Washington during a game in 1944.

WORTH A MILLION

After years of struggles, the Cardinals hit a low point in 1943 when they failed to win a single game. The 1944 season was even more difficult. World War II (1939–1945) required many young men to serve overseas, which in turn depleted the rosters of several NFL teams. With the Cardinals and Pittsburgh Steelers especially low on players, the teams were forced to combine for the 1944 season.

The team was known as "Card-Pitt." However, fans commonly adapted the name to be "the carpets," since the rest of the league walked all over the team that season. Card-Pitt went 0–10 and was outscored 328–108.

Whether playing as the Cardinals or as Card-Pitt, the team suffered its lowest points between 1943 and 1945. After a victory against the Detroit Lions on October 18, 1942, the Cardinals didn't

Cardinals owner Charles Bidwill, *right*, was inducted into the Pro Football Hall of Fame in 1967.

win another game until October 14, 1945. But just two years later, the Cardinals were back as championship contenders.

The Cardinals started building toward success in 1945 with the signing of quarterback Paul Christman. Then in 1946, fullback Pat Harder and halfback Elmer Angsman joined the club. Bidwill pulled out all the stops to get the last piece he believed his team needed. In 1947, he signed Georgia star running back Charley Trippi to what was then a high-paying contract of $100,000.

Running back Charley Trippi, *center*, poses with Bidwill, *left*, and head coach Jimmy Conzelman after signing with the Cardinals in 1947.

The value of the players that season earned them the nickname "the Million Dollar Backfield." However, Bidwill did not live to see his investment pay off. He died before the 1947 season, just months after signing Trippi. Ownership of the team then passed to Violet Bidwill. She became the first female owner of an NFL team.

The Million Dollar Backfield proved to be worth every penny as the Cardinals stormed through the 1947 season. By then, the NFL had divided into the East and West divisions. The Cardinals beat the Bears in the final game of the season to win the West Division. They then faced the Philadelphia Eagles, the East Division winners, for the NFL championship.

The Cardinals got to host the game. But in late December in Chicago, the field was frozen. The Cardinals decided to wear sneakers because their cleats would not dig in to the frozen ground.

***From top left to right*, Elmer Angsman, Paul Christman, Pat Harder, and Trippi, who made up the Million Dollar Backfield, leap over the offensive line during a photo shoot in 1947.**

That decision, and the Million Dollar Backfield, made the difference.

During the game, Christman completed only three passes. But Harder's blocking helped the Cardinals run wild. Angsman ran for two 70-yard touchdowns, and Trippi ran for one touchdown and scored another on a 75-yard punt return. The Cardinals beat the Eagles 28–21 to win their second NFL championship. "It's just too bad that Charley couldn't have seen this," Violet said afterward.

Angsman, *left*, presents the game ball to Violet Bidwill, *right*, and her son, Bill, *center*, after the Cardinals' NFL championship victory in 1947.

END OF AN ERA

The 1948 Cardinals were even better. They went 11–1 and made it back to the championship game. But this time, the Eagles got revenge in a 7–0 win in Philadelphia. It was the last time the Cardinals would make the playoffs while playing in Chicago.

The Cardinals had long been overshadowed by the Bears in Chicago. By the time the Cardinals won their second championship,

Defensive back Dick Lane, *top*, led the NFL with 10 interceptions during his first season with the Cardinals in 1954.

the Bears had already won seven. The Bears and their success were what most fans cared about. Even in the Cardinals' stellar 1948 season, they drew only one crowd of more than 30,000 fans when 52,000 came to watch them play the Bears.

The Cardinals' poor play over the next several seasons hurt attendance, even as the team attracted stars such as defensive back Dick "Night Train" Lane. Lane, who earned his nickname for the tremendous force of his tackles, made four Pro Bowls as a Cardinal. But the team had only one winning season with him, in 1956.

The Bidwill family was losing money running the Cardinals. Meanwhile, the NFL was looking at the city of St. Louis as a market for a new team. Although the Bidwills were reluctant to leave Chicago, the family moved the team to St. Louis before the 1960 season. In St. Louis, the Cardinals would again be second in popularity. But this time, it was because of a different major professional sports team.

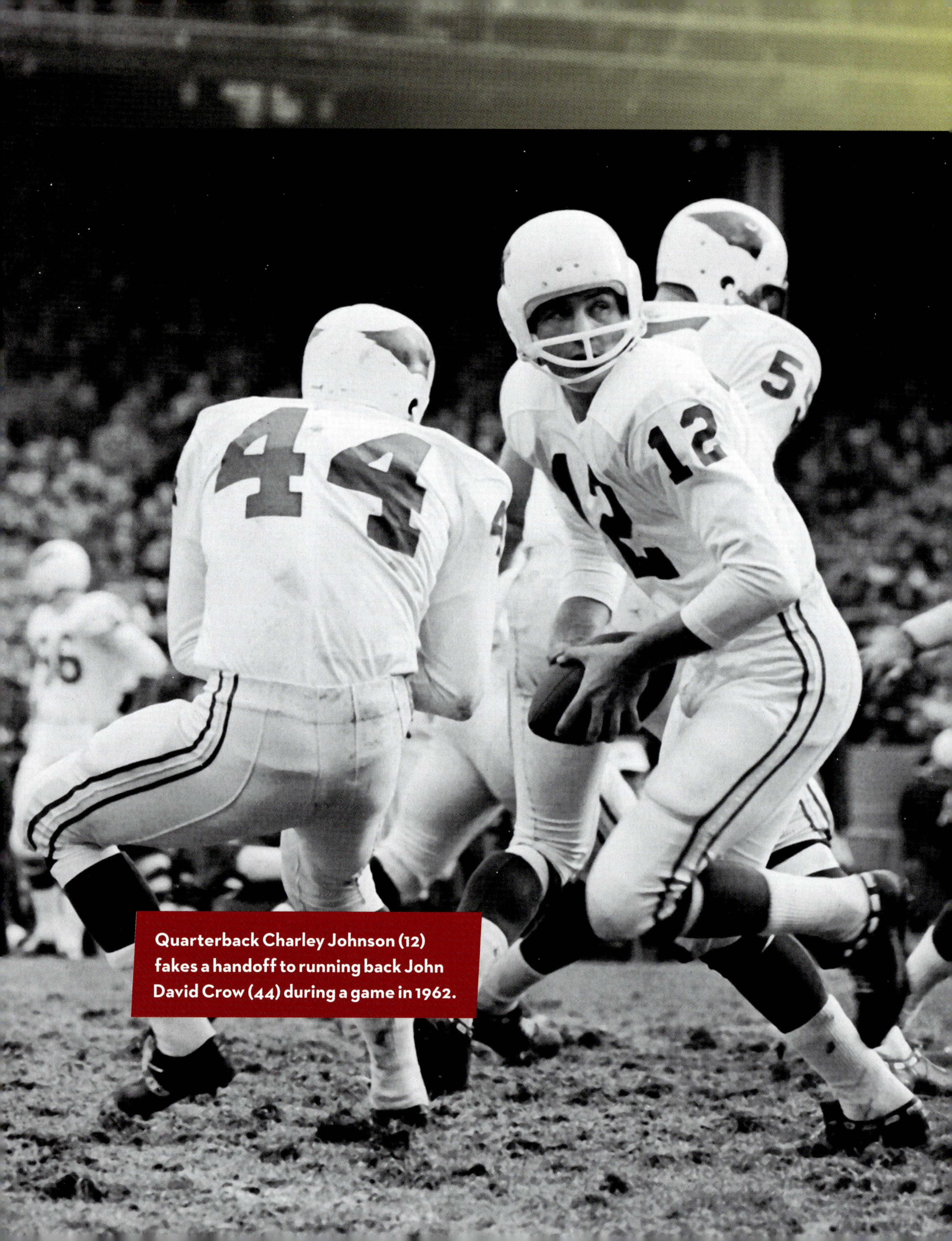

Quarterback Charley Johnson (12) fakes a handoff to running back John David Crow (44) during a game in 1962.

CHAPTER 3

ANOTHER ST. LOUIS CARDINALS

THE CARDINALS' MOVE TO ST. LOUIS WAS CONFUSING FOR SOME PEOPLE. This was because the city already had a team called the Cardinals. But that team played pro baseball.

As they did in Chicago, the Cardinals football team moved into a baseball stadium for home games. Busch Stadium was decades old by 1960. But the owners of the baseball Cardinals planned to build a new, modern stadium that could also accommodate football.

The Cardinals played their first NFL game in St. Louis on October 2, 1960. They lost 35–14 to the New York Giants. But it wasn't long after that the team started seeing some success. The Cardinals gradually assembled a strong core of young players throughout the early 1960s.

Tight end Jackie Smith, *in white*, caught 480 passes for the Cardinals between 1963 and 1977.

Wide receiver Sonny Randle made the move with the Cardinals from Chicago. He developed into a star in St. Louis. Randle set team records with 60 receiving touchdowns and 5,438 receiving yards across eight seasons with the Cardinals.

Passing to Randle during the early to mid-1960s was quarterback Charley Johnson. Johnson was one of the Cardinals' first draft picks after the move. While Johnson made just one Pro Bowl in his career, he became known for leading comebacks. From 1966 to 1968, Johnson led six comeback wins in the fourth quarter.

Johnson missed several games in 1967 and 1968 to serve in the military. Quarterback Jim Hart took over as the starter. He held the job for the next 15 years. In that time, Hart broke most of the team's single-season passing records, including the records for yards and touchdowns. Hart also had the single-season wins record and was known for leading comebacks. From 1974 to 1976, he led 10 game-winning drives.

Defensive back Roger Wehrli went to seven Pro Bowls in 14 seasons with the Cardinals after joining the team in 1969.

On defense, Larry Wilson was a nightmare for quarterbacks. An offensive and defensive player in college, Wilson cemented himself as a safety in the NFL. In an era when safeties usually did not rush the quarterback, Wilson's athleticism helped him get to the passer and deliver bruising sacks. He also terrorized quarterbacks with interceptions. Wilson had at least two of them in all 13 seasons of his Hall of Fame career.

The 1960s Cardinals posted several seasons with a winning record. In 1963 and 1964, they recorded nine wins, which they hadn't done since the 1940s. But the team kept coming up just short of the playoffs.

Safety Larry Wilson had a franchise-record 52 career interceptions in 13 seasons with the Cardinals.

THE GOVERNOR'S CUP

Much like their rivalry with the Bears in their Chicago years, the Cardinals had an in-state rival during their time in St. Louis. The Cardinals and Kansas City Chiefs played each other in the preseason every year from 1968 to 1987. They also met five times in the regular season. The winner each season was awarded a trophy known as the Missouri Governor's Cup. The Cardinals won the Cup seven times.

Meanwhile, the team underwent some off-field changes during the 1960s. Just two years into their new home, Violet Bidwill unexpectedly passed away. She left the team to her sons, Stormy and Bill. Stormy would later sell his share to Bill, who ran the team for nearly 50 years.

In 1966, the Cardinals entered a new era with the opening of their upgraded stadium. Although the Cardinals still had to share with a baseball team, the new Busch Stadium was designed for both football and baseball. It was the first time the team had a home built with football in mind. The brand-new stadium also sat nearly 50,000 fans. It provided the kind of home-field advantage the Cardinals never had in Chicago.

Head coach Don Coryell had a record of 42-27-1 in five seasons with the Cardinals.

AIR CORYELL

The hiring of head coach Don Coryell in 1973 helped improve the Cardinals' passing attack. At the time, most offenses were based around running the ball. But Coryell's offense, nicknamed "Air Coryell," prioritized passing. In 1969, when Coryell was head coach at San Diego State, his quarterback threw 14 more touchdown passes than any other college quarterback that year.

Receiver Mel Gray had 11 touchdown receptions in 1975.

The Cardinals had a 4–9–1 record in Coryell's first year as head coach. But the team recorded double-digit wins in each of the next three seasons. In 1974, the Cardinals won their first division title in 26 years. A lot of that success came from the offense.

The Air Coryell offense worked so well because of the talented players running it. Hart had a superstar receiver in Mel Gray, who led the NFL in touchdown receptions in 1975. The Cardinals didn't just pass, though. They also had a pair of star running backs in Terry Metcalf and Jim Otis. And they had key players blocking for Hart. In 1974, the Cardinals featured one of the best offensive lines in football. Players such as Conrad Dobler, Bob Young, and future Hall of Famer Dan Dierdorf helped keep Hart from getting sacked while creating big holes for the running backs to score.

The Cardinals' return to the playoffs looked promising early on. Playing a powerful Vikings team in Minnesota, Hart threw a touchdown pass to give the Cardinals a 7–0 lead in the second quarter. But the Vikings tied it up in the second and went on to beat the Cardinals 30–14.

Quarterback Jim Hart unloads a pass against the Baltimore Colts during a game in 1978.

The 1975 Cardinals improved by one win, going 11–3 to win another division title. However, the playoff results were the same. In the divisional round, the Los Angeles Rams scored early and often, racing out to a 21–0 lead. A touchdown pass from Hart to Gray made it 28–16 in the third quarter, but that was as close as the Cardinals got in another disappointing playoff loss.

A 10-win season followed for the Cardinals in 1976. But this time, it wasn't enough for the team to win its third straight division title. St. Louis slipped to a 7–7 record in 1977, which was the last for Coryell as the Cardinals' head coach. Coryell had expressed his unhappiness with the direction of the franchise, leading Bill Bidwill to fire him after the 1977 season.

HEADING FARTHER SOUTHWEST

As the Air Coryell years came to an end, a new star emerged for the Cardinals in 1979. Running back Ottis Anderson was the team's top pick in that year's NFL Draft. In his first game, he ran for 193 yards against the Dallas Cowboys.

Anderson was a powerful and fast runner. He ran for 1,605 yards in his rookie season while also scoring 10 total touchdowns. Anderson surpassed 1,000 rushing yards in five of his first six seasons. By the time his career with the Cardinals came to an end in 1986, he held all the team's major rushing records.

As Anderson finished his time in St. Louis, the Cardinals' future in the city was unclear. The formerly state-of-the-art Busch Stadium was beginning to show its age, and the Cardinals were tired of sharing it with the baseball Cardinals. Bidwill was trying to get a new stadium built in St. Louis, but the team and the city could not come to an agreement.

As Bidwill looked for a new home during the 1987 season, Phoenix emerged as a front-runner. The Cardinals played their last game in St. Louis on December 13 of that year. Just a few months later, the Cardinals were officially moving to the desert.

Running back Ottis Anderson rushed for almost 8,000 yards in eight seasons with the Cardinals.

Quarterback Neil Lomax fires a pass during the Cardinals' first home game in Arizona on September 15, 1988.

CHAPTER 4

SUPER IN THE DESERT

The Cardinals shared Chicago with a more popular football team. Then they shared St. Louis with a more popular baseball team. In Arizona, they had a chance to be the biggest show in town. The only major professional team in Phoenix in 1988 was the Phoenix Suns of the National Basketball Association. The Suns were popular, but fans in the city had been wanting a pro football team for years. "We were welcomed as conquering heroes here in Phoenix," said Cardinals fullback Ron Wolfley.

Although the Cardinals played at the home of the Arizona State college football team in nearby Tempe, they adopted the name Phoenix Cardinals. Playing at Sun Devil Stadium was meant to be temporary. The Cardinals still hoped to build their own stadium.

EARLY THRILLS AND STRUGGLES

The Cardinals started the 1988 season on a low note, losing their opener on the road to the Cincinnati Bengals. Then they fell in their first home game the following week, this time to the Dallas Cowboys. The Cardinals rebounded to win their next four games. By the time the powerful San Francisco 49ers came to Arizona for a big Week 10 game, the Cardinals stood 5–4.

The 49ers were loaded with future Hall of Famers, and they showed their might by going ahead 23–0 in the third quarter. After that, Cardinals fans started leaving. Wolfley later said, "I remember I got up and hung over the fence for the first and only time of my

The Cardinals and San Francisco 49ers face off in the Week 10 game of the 1988 season.

NFL career. . . . And I was yelling at [the fans], 'You're gonna miss the greatest comeback in the history of this team!'"

Quarterback Neil Lomax, who had come with the team from St. Louis, started the comeback with a touchdown pass later in the third. A field goal and another touchdown from the Cardinals brought the score to 23–17 in the fourth quarter. They just needed a defensive stop for a chance at a game-winning drive.

On third-and-four, 49ers quarterback Steve Young tried to run for a first down, but Cardinals linebacker E. J. Junior met him with a big hit just short of the first down marker. This forced the 49ers to punt. Lomax then led the Cardinals down the field in only six plays. With his last throw, he hit receiver Roy Green for a 9-yard touchdown to lift the Cardinals to a 24–23 victory.

However, the win proved to be the high note of the season, as the Cardinals lost five of their last six games to finish 7–9. Fans hoped it was a year to build on. Instead, the Cardinals didn't post a winning record in their first 10 seasons in Arizona.

PLAYOFF BREAKTHROUGH

In 1994, the team changed its name to the Arizona Cardinals to appeal to more fans across the state. Three years later, the Cardinals made another decision they hoped would spur local interest when they drafted Jake Plummer. The quarterback was coming off a great

Quarterback Jake Plummer (16) led the Cardinals to five fourth-quarter comeback wins in 1998.

season at Arizona State, having led the Sun Devils to an 11-1 record in 1996. In keeping Plummer local, the Cardinals hoped his strong arm and playmaking abilities could help turn the city's professional team into winners, too.

The winning ways didn't come right away, though. Plummer struggled as a rookie, and the Cardinals finished 4-12. Not much was expected of the team in 1998. An 0-2 start seemed to prove that. But the defense, led by future Hall of Fame defensive back Aeneas Williams, helped keep the Cardinals in a lot of close games. Arizona went into the final game of the season needing a win over the San Diego Chargers to make the playoffs.

A crowd of more than 71,000 fans packed into Sun Devil Stadium hoping to witness Cardinals history. The game featured very little scoring. The Cardinals went ahead early on a touchdown and led

In 10 seasons with the Cardinals, defensive back Aeneas Williams recorded 46 interceptions. Six of those were returned for touchdowns, which is a team record.

Fans attempt to tear down the goalpost after the Cardinals beat the San Diego Chargers in 1998 to clinch a playoff berth.

13–3 going into the fourth quarter. However, the Chargers tied the game 13–13 with just 22 seconds remaining.

On the kickoff, the Cardinals advanced the ball to the Chargers' 44-yard line. Plummer threw a 10-yard pass to put the team in field-goal position. Then Cardinals kicker Chris Jacke lined up for a 52-yard field-goal attempt. The ball started going right but slowly curved back and sailed through the uprights to give the Cardinals a 16–13 win and a spot in the playoffs. Thousands of fans, including owner Bill Bidwill, flooded onto the field in celebration.

But the job wasn't done yet. The Cardinals then set out to secure their first playoff win in more than 50 years. The team went on the road in the wild-card round to face the Dallas Cowboys, who had beaten the Cardinals twice already during the 1998 regular season. But Arizona showed early in the game that it was a different team.

Plummer threw a touchdown pass in the first quarter, and the team never looked back. The defense shut out the Cowboys until late in the game as the Cardinals won 20–7.

The Minnesota Vikings awaited Arizona in the next round. The Vikings had set a new NFL scoring record that season, and by halftime, they led 24–7. Two rushing touchdowns from Arizona running back Mario Bates in the second half got the Cardinals within 13 points, but they never got any closer in a 41–21 loss. The Cardinals' magical run was over. And they struggled to match that success in the following seasons. But the 1998 team had given fans amazing moments they hadn't seen in several years.

Running back Adrian Murrell spikes the ball after scoring a touchdown against the Dallas Cowboys in the playoffs after the 1998 season.

FINALLY HOME

When the Cardinals moved to Arizona, they planned to play at Sun Devil Stadium for only a short time until they built a stadium of their own. But a financial crisis in Arizona meant there was no money available from the state to contribute to a new stadium. The project kept being pushed out further into the future. Finally, in 2000, Arizona voters approved funding for a new home for the Cardinals, and construction began three years later.

While their new stadium was being built, the Cardinals transformed their on-field look with a major redesign of their uniforms in 2005. The Cardinals' logo changed to look sleeker and meaner. The uniforms were also updated with a modern styling to signify a new era.

Then, in 2006, the team moved into their new stadium. Located in nearby Glendale, the stadium featured a retractable roof to keep out the desert sun on hot days

PAT TILLMAN

Safety Pat Tillman had starred at Arizona State before the Cardinals picked him in the seventh round of the 1997 NFL Draft. Despite his low draft position, Tillman immediately became a starting safety as a rookie. But in 2002, Tillman walked away from the NFL to serve in the military. He was killed in action while fighting in Afghanistan in 2004. The Cardinals honored Tillman's memory by retiring his uniform, No. 40.

Pat Tillman had three interceptions and 2 1/2 sacks during his career.

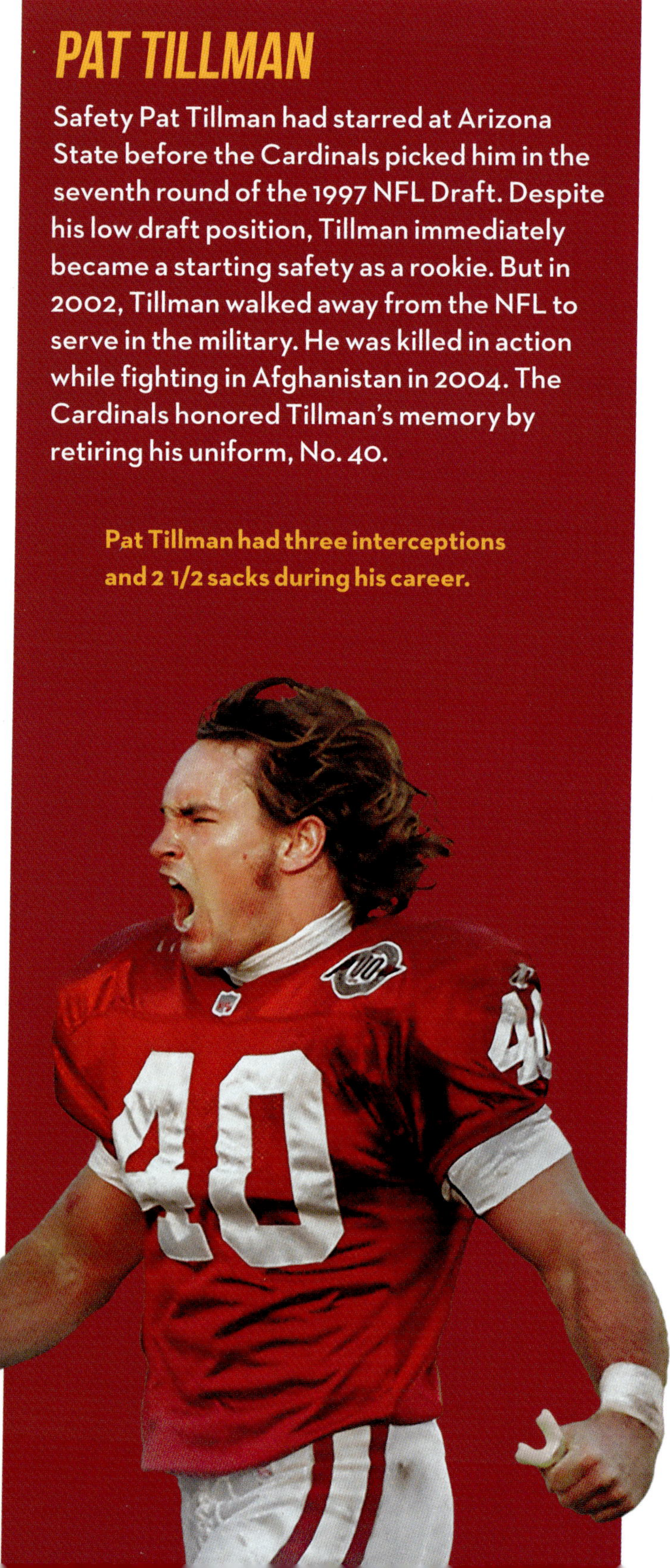

along with a natural grass field. But most importantly, the stadium was a home built just for the Cardinals.

THE BIRDS TAKE FLIGHT

While the Cardinals were overhauling their look and home, they were building up their roster as well. Larry Fitzgerald arrived as the Cardinals' top pick in the 2004 draft and quickly began developing into one of the top receivers in the NFL. The team also had exciting changes at quarterback.

In 2005, the team signed veteran quarterback Kurt Warner. A savvy passer, Warner had led the St. Louis Rams to a pair of Super Bowls, winning one of them while also earning two NFL Most Valuable Player (MVP) Awards. The Cardinals had never had a quarterback with that sort of winning experience.

Receiver Larry Fitzgerald (11) played all 17 years of his pro career with the Cardinals.

However, after a 5–11 season in 2005, the Cardinals picked up another highly-touted quarterback in Matt Leinart during the 2006 NFL Draft.

Coming off a storied career at the University of Southern California (USC), Leinart grabbed the starting job in Week 5 of his rookie season. But when the young quarterback began struggling early in the 2007 season, Warner came on in relief and did well. Leinart later got injured, and Warner led the team to an 8–8 record, throwing 27 touchdowns in 14 games.

Neither quarterback was assured of starting in 2008. After training camp and preseason, head coach Ken Whisenhunt decided to go with the veteran Warner. The move paid off as Warner played like an MVP again. He set a Cardinals record with 30 touchdown passes in 2008. And Warner had a trio of receivers with 1,000 yards in Fitzgerald, Anquan Boldin, and Steve Breaston.

Even with a talented offense, the Cardinals barely had a winning record in 2008 at 9–7. However, it was good enough to not only make the playoffs but also give the Cardinals their first division title since 1975. And the team hosted its first playoff game since 1947.

Cardinals fans were more than ready for a game 60 years in the making. And they got to see a huge performance from Fitzgerald, who caught six passes for 101 yards and a touchdown during the 30–24 win over the Atlanta Falcons. Then the Cardinals went on

In 2008, Kurt Warner (13) became the second Cardinals quarterback to top 4,000 passing yards in a season when he threw for 4,583.

Arizona fans cheer during the playoff game between the Cardinals and Carolina Panthers after the 2008 season.

the road and crushed the Carolina Panthers 33–13 in the divisional round. The following week, Arizona hosted the National Football Conference (NFC) title game against the Philadelphia Eagles, with a trip to the Super Bowl on the line.

Fitzgerald caught three touchdowns in the first half, including a 62-yard bomb, to help the Cardinals go up 24–6 at halftime. But in the second half, the Eagles stormed back. They scored three touchdowns in a row to take a 25–24 lead in the fourth quarter.

The Cardinals did not panic, though. "We were like, 'We got the ball last, we'll go down and score,'" said Breaston.

On the next Cardinals possession, Warner marched his team down the field. Facing fourth-and-inches from the Philadelphia 49-yard line, Arizona running back Tim Hightower took the ball and sprinted to the right. Eagles defenders closed in, but Hightower outran them to get the first down.

Hightower came up big again later in the drive. On third down from the 8-yard line, Warner looked to pass. He found Hightower, who fought his way through defenders to the goal line for a touchdown. The defense then shut down any hope for an Eagles comeback. The 32–25 victory meant the Cardinals were finally heading to their first Super Bowl.

Arizona players dump Gatorade on head coach Ken Whisenhunt after the team defeated the Philadelphia Eagles in the NFC title game in January 2009.

FORTY-TWO SECONDS

Super Bowl XLIII brought a matchup between the NFL's least accomplished and most accomplished teams. The Pittsburgh Steelers had won four Super Bowls in the 1970s. They were regular contenders in the 1990s and early 2000s, winning their fifth title in 2005. Through three quarters against Arizona, the Steelers built a 20–7 lead. But the Cardinals weren't giving up. "We weren't going to throw in the towel," said defensive lineman Bertrand Berry.

> **"WE WEREN'T GOING TO THROW IN THE TOWEL."**
>
> **—BERTRAND BERRY**

The combo of Fitzgerald and Warner got things going on offense. With 7:41 to go, Warner connected with Fitzgerald for a 1-yard touchdown. Minutes later, the Steelers were backed up on their own 1-yard line. Pittsburgh quarterback Ben Roethlisberger completed a 19-yard pass, but there was a flag on the play. A penalty against the Steelers in the end zone resulted in a safety. With those two points, Arizona cut the lead to 20–16. The Cardinals also got the ball back with a chance to take the lead.

Warner didn't need much time. On the second play of the next drive, he dropped back and saw Fitzgerald running down the middle of the field. Warner hit the receiver with a pass, and Fitzgerald did the rest. He turned up the field, outrunning every Steelers defender who tried to catch him. None of them got close as Fitzgerald ran into the end zone for a 64-yard touchdown to put the Cardinals up 23–20.

There was one problem, though. Roethlisberger and Pittsburgh had 2:30 left to either tie the game or go ahead on a touchdown. Starting from their own 22-yard line, the Steelers got to work.

Fitzgerald sprints away from the Pittsburgh Steelers' defense for a touchdown in Super Bowl XLIII on February 1, 2009.

Roethlisberger led the Steelers down the field until they reached the Arizona 6-yard line.

With 48 seconds remaining, Steelers receiver Santonio Holmes ran to the corner of the end zone. Roethlisberger threw a pass toward the back of the end zone that looked uncatchable. But Holmes stretched out to grab it while just barely getting his toes down inbounds. The iconic play put the Steelers back on top with just 42 seconds left. The Cardinals were unable to respond and lost 27–23. The loss was heartbreaking for the Cardinals, but the team and its fans hoped it could be built upon in seasons to come.

The catch by Steelers receiver Santonio Holmes (10) denied the Cardinals their first Super Bowl title.

Linebacker Karlos Dansby recovers a fumble in the Cardinals' playoff game against the Green Bay Packers after the 2009 season.

CHAPTER 5

FLYING HIGH

ANY HOPE OF THE CARDINALS REPEATING THEIR 2008 SUCCESS GOT A big boost when Kurt Warner re-signed for the 2009 season. Arizona followed up its Super Bowl season by going 10–6. Warner then treated the home crowd to one of the best performances of his career. During the team's wild-card matchup with the Green Bay Packers in the playoffs, Warner tossed five touchdown passes. But the veteran quarterback wasn't the only standout of the high-scoring game.

The Packers and Cardinals were tied 45–45 at the end of the fourth quarter to send the game into overtime. Green Bay started with the ball, and about one minute in, Arizona defensive back Michael Adams sacked Packers quarterback Aaron Rodgers. Rodgers fumbled the ball, and Cardinals linebacker Karlos Dansby recovered it and ran 17 yards for the game-winning touchdown. The Cardinals' 51–45 overtime victory against the Packers was the highest-scoring playoff game in NFL history.

However, the Cardinals' quest for a repeat Super Bowl appearance ended in a 45–14 loss to the New Orleans Saints in the divisional round. Warner, nearing 40 years old, retired after the 2009 season. The Cardinals still had plenty of talented weapons on offense, but they struggled to replace Warner. After missing the playoffs for four years in a row, head coach Ken Whisenhunt was fired after the 2012 season.

PALMER POWER

New head coach Bruce Arians quickly became a fan favorite for his aggressive play calling. He favored taking risks for big rewards rather than playing it safe. The Cardinals also got him a capable quarterback to work with in veteran Carson Palmer. Playing in Arians's system, Palmer led the Cardinals to some of their winningest seasons in team history.

After going 10–6 in 2013 but missing the playoffs, Arizona came back strong with an 11–5 record in 2014, despite Palmer being hurt for most of the season. This time, the team made it to the playoffs. The Cardinals were down to third-string

Bruce Arians led the Cardinals to the playoffs twice in five seasons as their head coach.

Behind quarterback Carson Palmer's passing, Arizona set a franchise record for wins with 13 in 2015.

quarterback Ryan Lindley for their wild-card round game against the Carolina Panthers. Lindley threw two interceptions as the Cardinals lost 27–16.

By win total, 2015 was the best season in Cardinals history. A healthy Palmer set team passing records with 4,671 yards and 35 touchdowns. Arizona also won 13 games, which was the second-most in the NFL that season.

After a first-round bye in the playoffs, the Cardinals faced the Packers in the divisional round. A back-and-forth game went to overtime tied 20–20. The Cardinals started with the ball in extra time. As a defender closed in on Palmer on the first play, the quarterback quickly spun to his right. He got free, found Fitzgerald wide-open, and fired a pass to him. Fitzgerald then turned on his speed, running away from multiple Packers defenders. One finally caught him at the 5-yard line, but the Cardinals were in business.

Larry Fitzgerald scores the winning touchdown in the playoff game against the Green Bay Packers after the 2015 season.

Just two plays later, Palmer found Fitzgerald again. This time, Palmer tossed a quick flip to the receiver. Fitzgerald ran up the middle for the game-winning score. The 26–20 overtime victory moved Arizona on to the NFC Championship Game.

However, the Cardinals' hope for another Super Bowl appearance ended there. Arizona faced the Panthers for a second straight year in the playoffs. And once again, the Cardinals lost, this time by a crushing 49–15 defeat. Palmer was not as sharp, throwing four interceptions.

Palmer and the Cardinals hoped to build on their success in 2016. Despite Palmer having another 4,000-yard passing season, the team struggled, winning just seven games. Another injury-filled season for Palmer followed in 2017. Both he and Arians retired after that.

Defensive end Chandler Jones set the Cardinals record for career sacks with 71 1/2 between 2016 and 2021.

A NEW HOPE

The Cardinals' search for a new coach and quarterback led to a series of disappointing seasons. Head coach Steve Wilks lasted just one season as Arizona went 3–13 in 2018. It was the team's worst record since 2000. However, that losing record meant the team got the top pick in the 2019 NFL Draft. The Cardinals used that pick to select quarterback Kyler Murray from Oklahoma. Murray had won the Heisman Trophy in 2018 as college football's best player.

Murray's athleticism and passing ability were clear. But some people worried that at 5 feet, 10 inches tall, he was too short to be an NFL star. The Cardinals paired Murray with a new head coach in Kliff Kingsbury, who was known for his exciting, high-scoring offenses while serving as head coach for Texas Tech. The Cardinals hoped Kingsbury would do the same for them.

Kyler Murray, *in white*, dives for a touchdown during a game against the Cincinnati Bengals in 2019.

Murray earned his chance to start right away. In his NFL debut, he threw for two touchdowns and more than 300 yards. Jake Plummer was the only other rookie quarterback to reach those marks in team history.

In Week 2, Murray passed for 349 yards. Three weeks later, he showed off both his passing and running ability by passing for

LARRY THE G.O.A.T.

Larry Fitzgerald retired after the 2020 season as one of the greatest Cardinals in history. He held all the team's major receiving records, in many cases by a huge margin. His 17,492 receiving yards were more than double of any other player. He was also at his best in the playoffs. In nine career playoff games, Fitzgerald had 942 receiving yards and 10 touchdowns.

Fitzgerald retired with the second-most receptions in NFL history with 1,432.

253 yards and running for 93 more with a touchdown. After the season, Murray was named the NFL's Offensive Rookie of the Year. Although the Cardinals won just five games that season, fans felt confident they had found their quarterback of the future.

FINDING THE RIGHT FIT

Arizona's "Hail Murray" play became an early highlight of Murray's career and one of the top plays of 2020. The win against the Buffalo Bills moved the Cardinals to 6-3. However, they faded down the homestretch of the season and missed the playoffs. That also marked Fitzgerald's final season, as he decided to retire.

Much like they had in 2020, the Cardinals started off hot in 2021. Murray was playing even better that season. He was considered a likely candidate

Linebacker Markus Golden (44) takes down Los Angeles Rams quarterback Matthew Stafford during a playoff game in January 2022.

for MVP. "Since [Kyler Murray has] been here, all he's done is gotten us better as a team and led the way," said Cardinals wide receiver Christian Kirk.

Despite dealing with an injury, Murray led the Cardinals to the playoffs with an 11-6 record.

"SINCE [KYLER MURRAY HAS] BEEN HERE, ALL HE'S DONE IS GOTTEN US BETTER AS A TEAM AND LED THE WAY."

—CHRISTIAN KIRK

CARDINALS TROPHY CASE

SUPER BOWL CHAMPIONSHIPS: 0

NFL CHAMPIONSHIPS: 2

1925, 1947

CONFERENCE CHAMPIONSHIPS: 3

1947, 1948, 2008

DIVISION TITLES: 5

NFC East: 1974, 1975
NFC West: 2008, 2009, 2015

All stats are through the 2024 season.

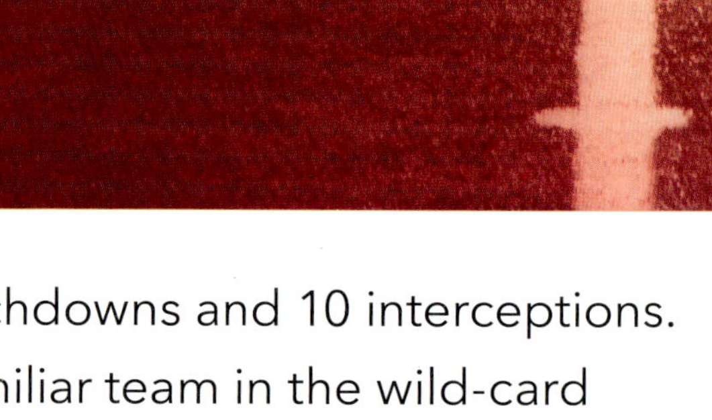

He threw for 3,787 yards with 24 touchdowns and 10 interceptions. Murray and the Cardinals faced a familiar team in the wild-card round of the playoffs. It was the division rival Los Angeles Rams.

Murray hoped to make a big splash in his first playoff game. Instead, he suffered one of the worst performances of his career.

Wide receiver Marvin Harrison Jr., *in red*, scored his first two professional touchdowns in Week 2 of the 2024 season.

The quarterback threw for just 137 yards with no touchdowns and two interceptions. The Cardinals lost 34–11 to end their season.

After a disappointing 4–13 season in 2022, Kingsbury was fired. The Cardinals then hired Jonathan Gannon, only to have another 4–13 season in 2023. To try to turn things around, Arizona paired Murray with the top receiver in the 2024 NFL Draft.

Former Ohio State star Marvin Harrison Jr. impressed fans as a rookie, hauling in eight touchdown catches. Meanwhile, third-year tight end Trey McBride caught a career-high 111 passes. While those offensive weapons helped the Cardinals improve to 8–9 in 2024, they still missed the playoffs. Even so, fans hoped the team's talented offensive core could lead the Cardinals to success for years to come.

TIMELINE

1898
The Cardinals are founded as the Morgan Athletic Club on the South Side of Chicago.

1920
The Racine Cardinals become original members of the APFA, the league that becomes the NFL.

1925
With the best record in the league, the Chicago Cardinals are named NFL champions for the first time.

1933
Chicago lawyer Charles Bidwill buys the Cardinals.

1944
Due to a shortage of players because of World War II, the Cardinals merge with the Pittsburgh Steelers for one season.

1947
A win against the Philadelphia Eagles gives the Cardinals a second NFL championship.

1960
Due to poor attendance and financial losses, the Cardinals move to St. Louis.

1974
Don Coryell's Cardinals win their first of two consecutive division titles in St. Louis.

1988
The Cardinals announce their move to Phoenix.

1998
Quarterback Jake Plummer leads the Cardinals to the playoffs and an upset win over the Dallas Cowboys.

2006
The Cardinals open their first football-only home stadium in franchise history.

2009
Kurt Warner leads the Cardinals to their first Super Bowl on February 1, but they lose to the Pittsburgh Steelers.

2015
Arizona sets a team record with 13 wins.

2024
The Cardinals draft wide receiver Marvin Harrison Jr. to play alongside standout quarterback Kyler Murray.

GLOSSARY

amateur—a person who plays a sport without getting paid.

comeback—a big rally after falling behind.

conference—a subset of teams within a sports league.

debut—first appearance.

draft—a system that allows teams to acquire new players coming into a league.

era—a period of time in history.

franchise—an entire sports organization.

fumble—losing the ball and allowing the opponent a chance to recover it.

iconic—well known for excellence.

interception—a pass that is caught by a defensive player.

Pro Bowl—a postseason competition that the NFL's all-stars are invited to compete in.

professional—a person who gets paid to perform.

retire—to end one's career.

retractable—able to be opened or closed.

rival—an opponent with whom a player or team has a fierce and ongoing competition.

rookie—a professional athlete in his or her first year of competition.

roster—a list of players who make up a team.

sack—a tackle of the quarterback behind the line of scrimmage before he can pass the ball.

safety—a score of two points for a team when its opponent is unable to advance the ball out of its own end zone.

scramble—to run around with the ball behind the line of scrimmage while looking for an open receiver.

third-string—a player who is the third choice for a certain position on a team.

upright—the vertical portion of the goalpost.

veteran—someone who has played for many years.

ONLINE RESOURCES

To learn more about the Arizona Cardinals, please visit **abdobooklinks.com** or scan this QR code. These links are routinely monitored and updated to provide the most current information available.

INDEX